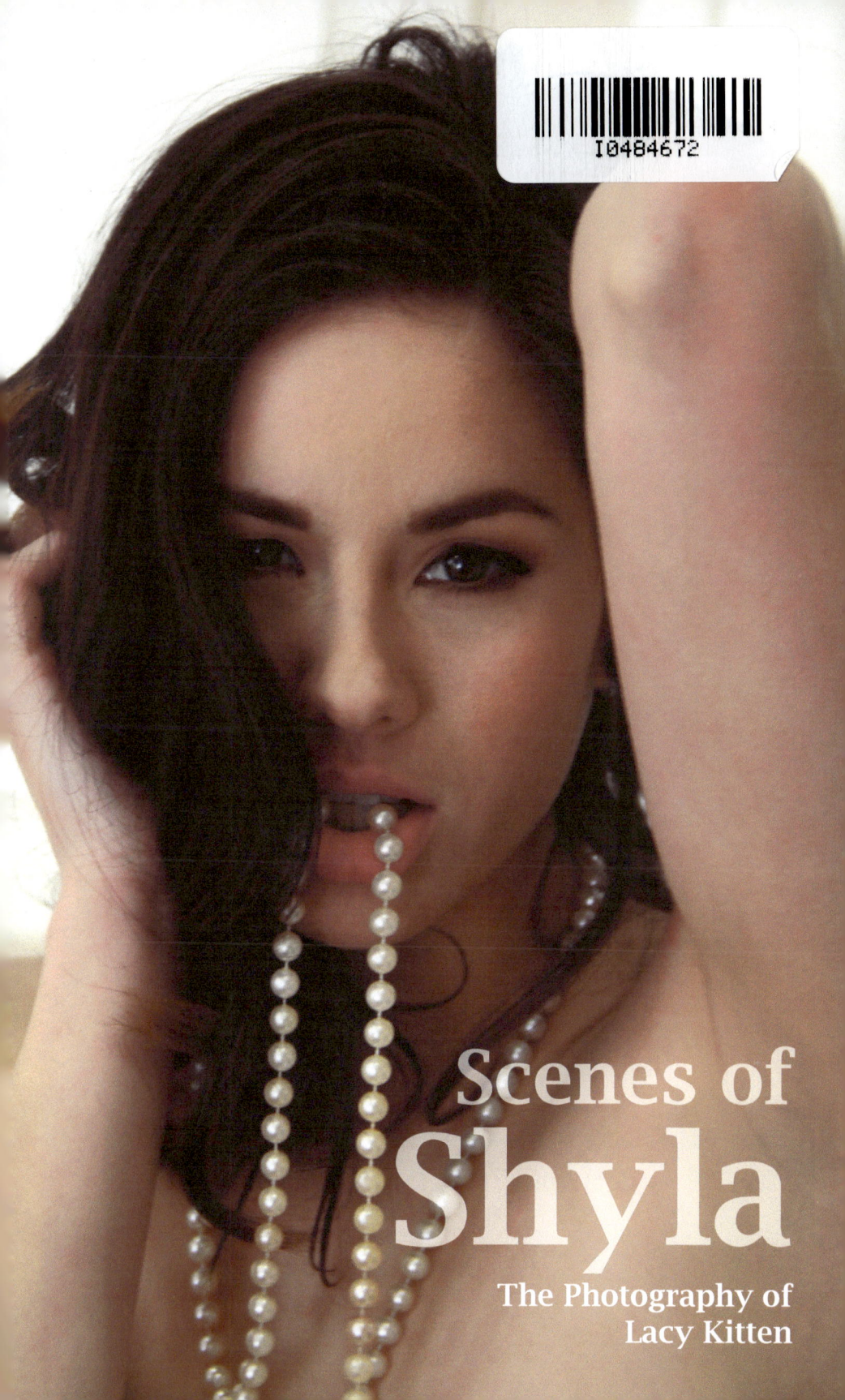

Scenes of
Shyla

The Photography of
Lacy Kitten

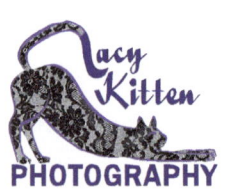

I know there are a million things pulling at your attention,
thank you for spending some time with my book.

This book is dedicated to all the fans
who appreciate the beauty and special qualities of Shyla Jennings.

A special thanks to Shyla Jennings for being
such a beautiful soul and a joy to work with.

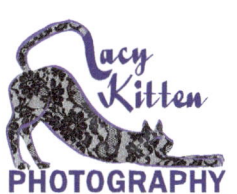

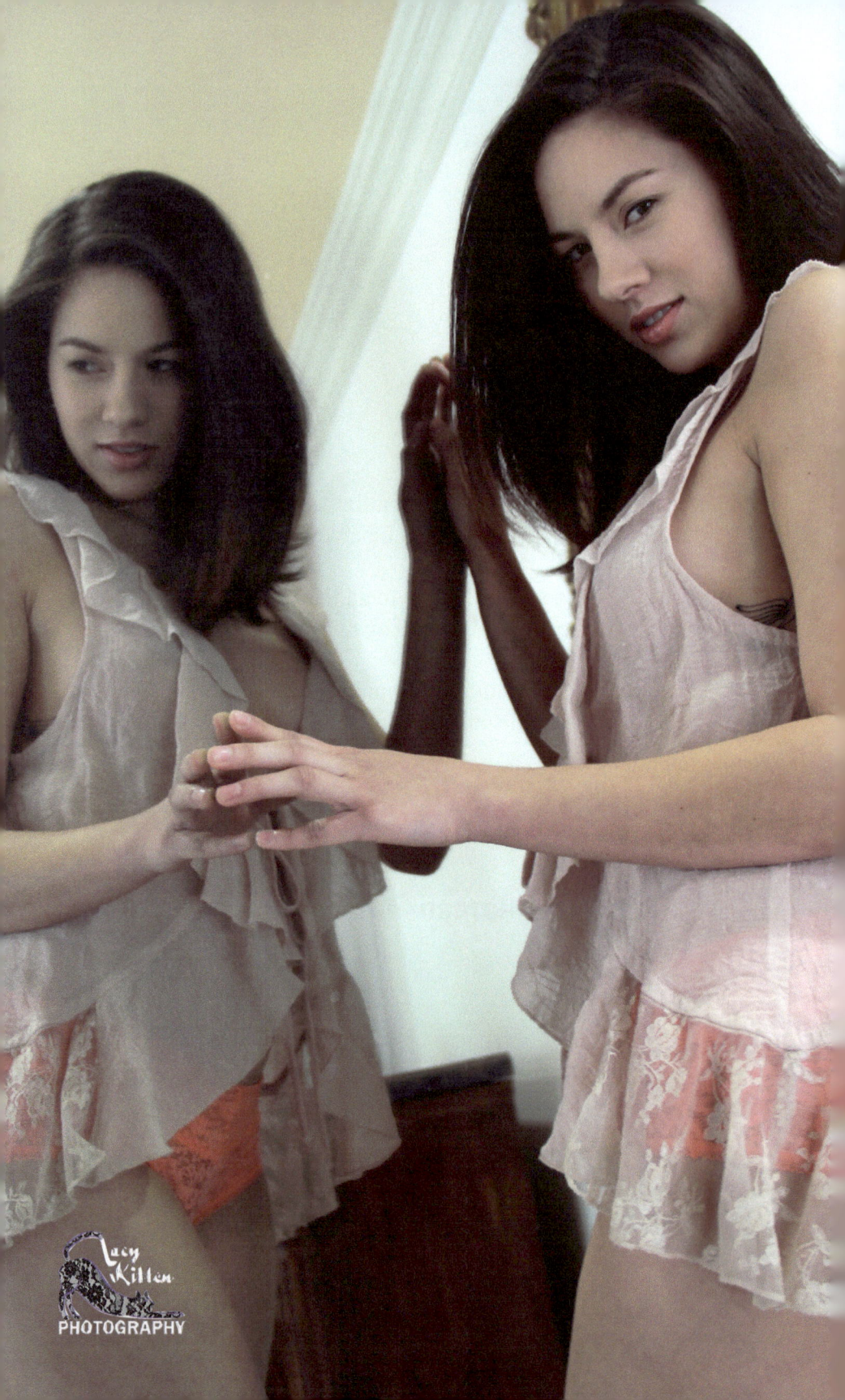

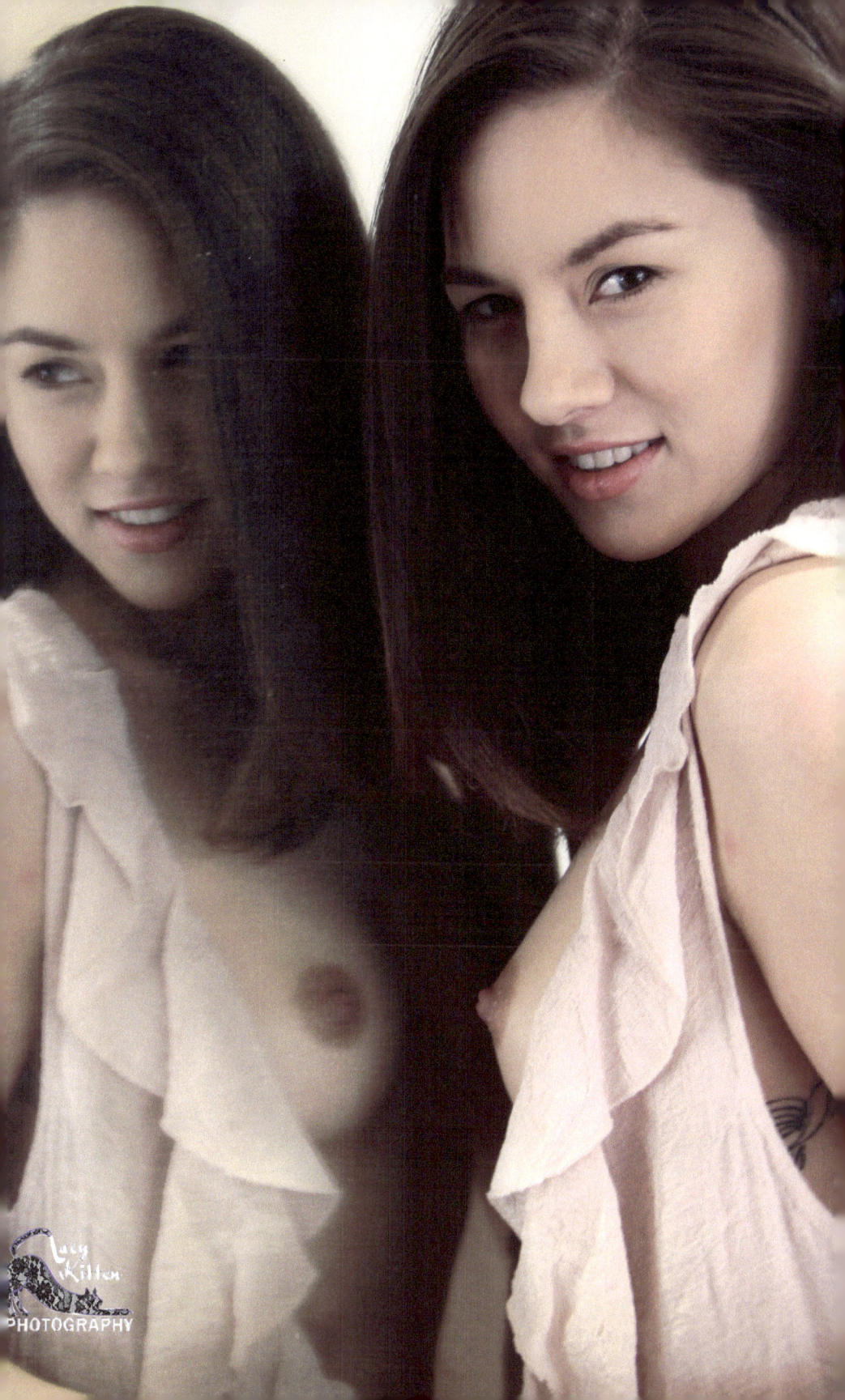

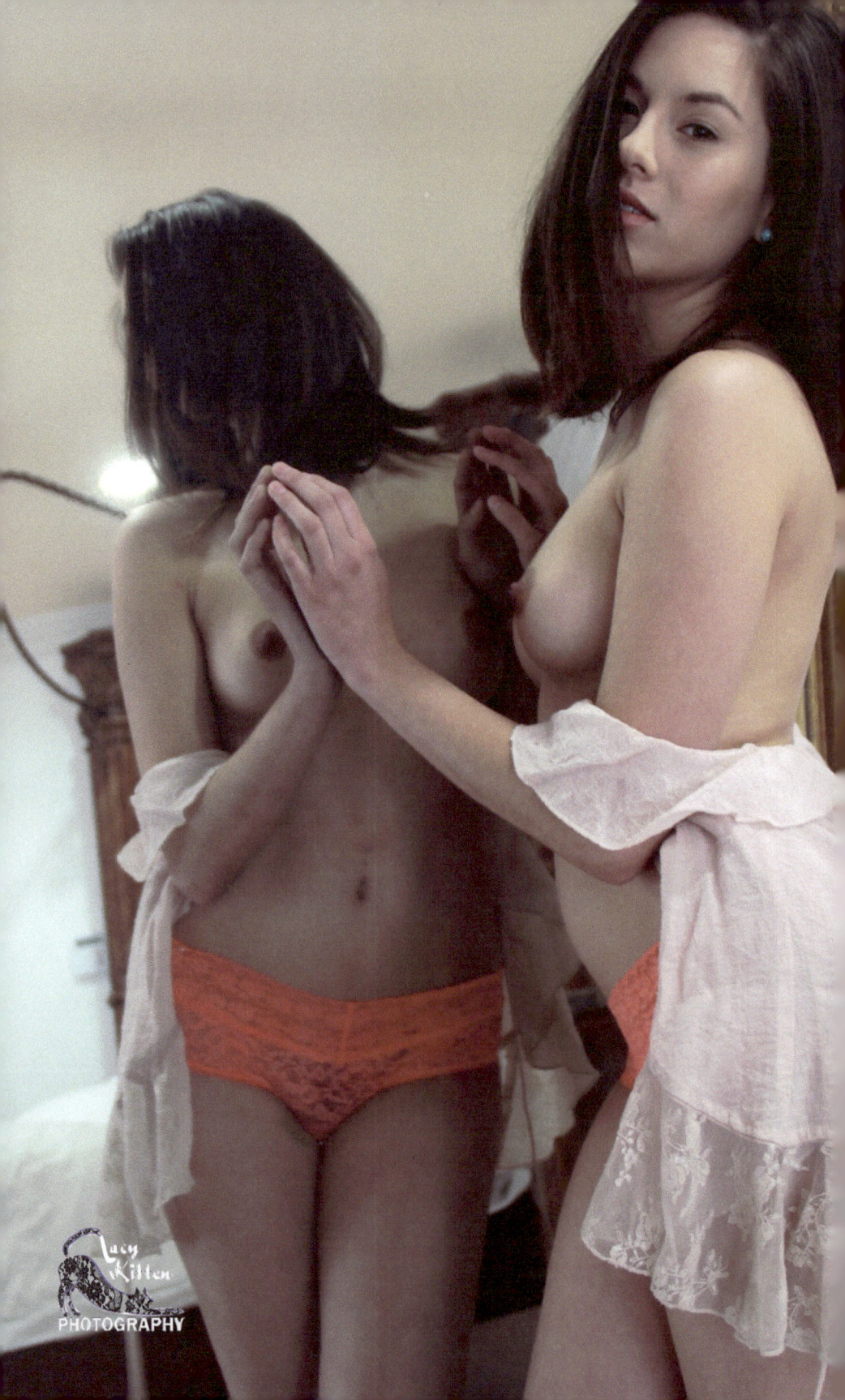

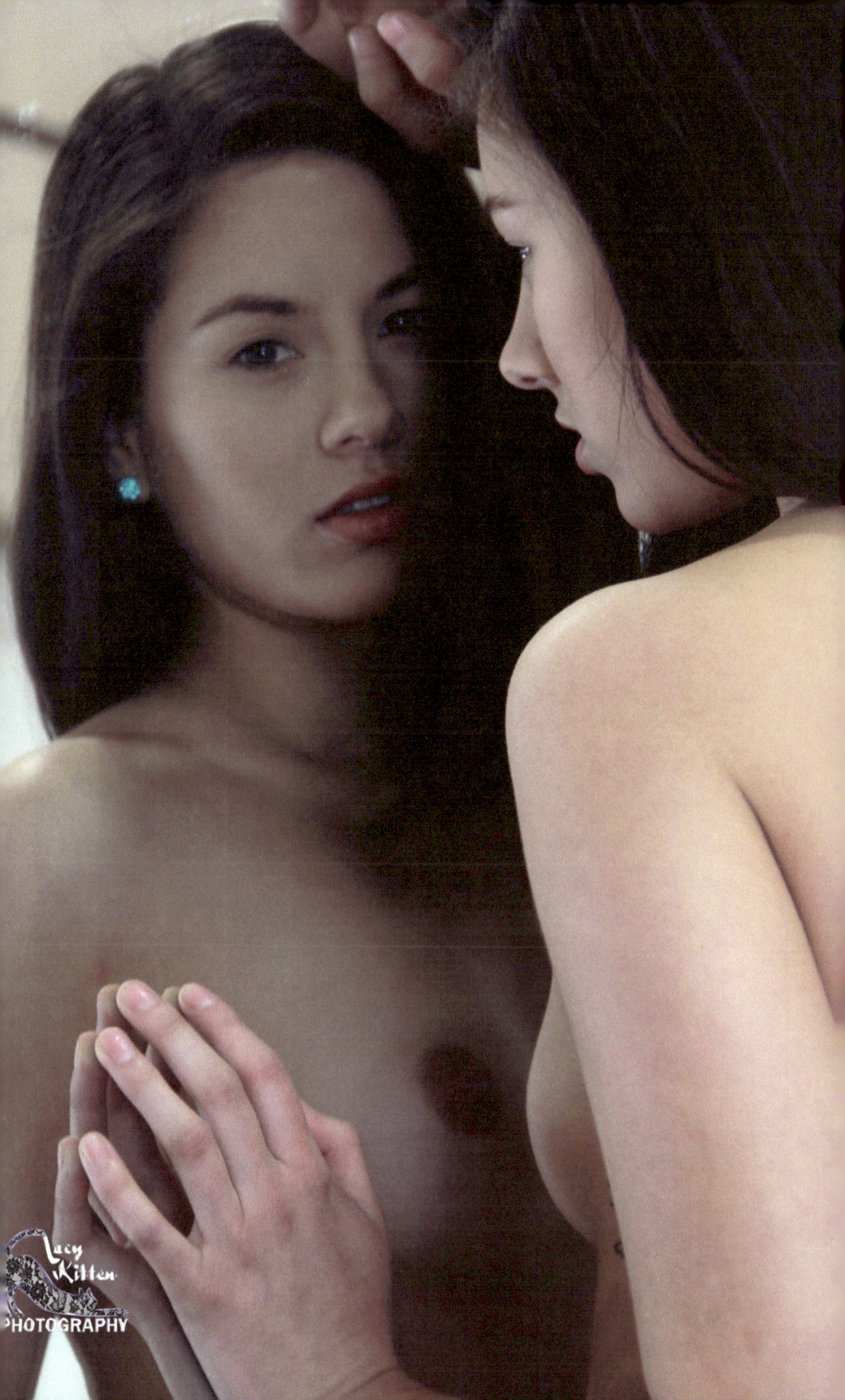

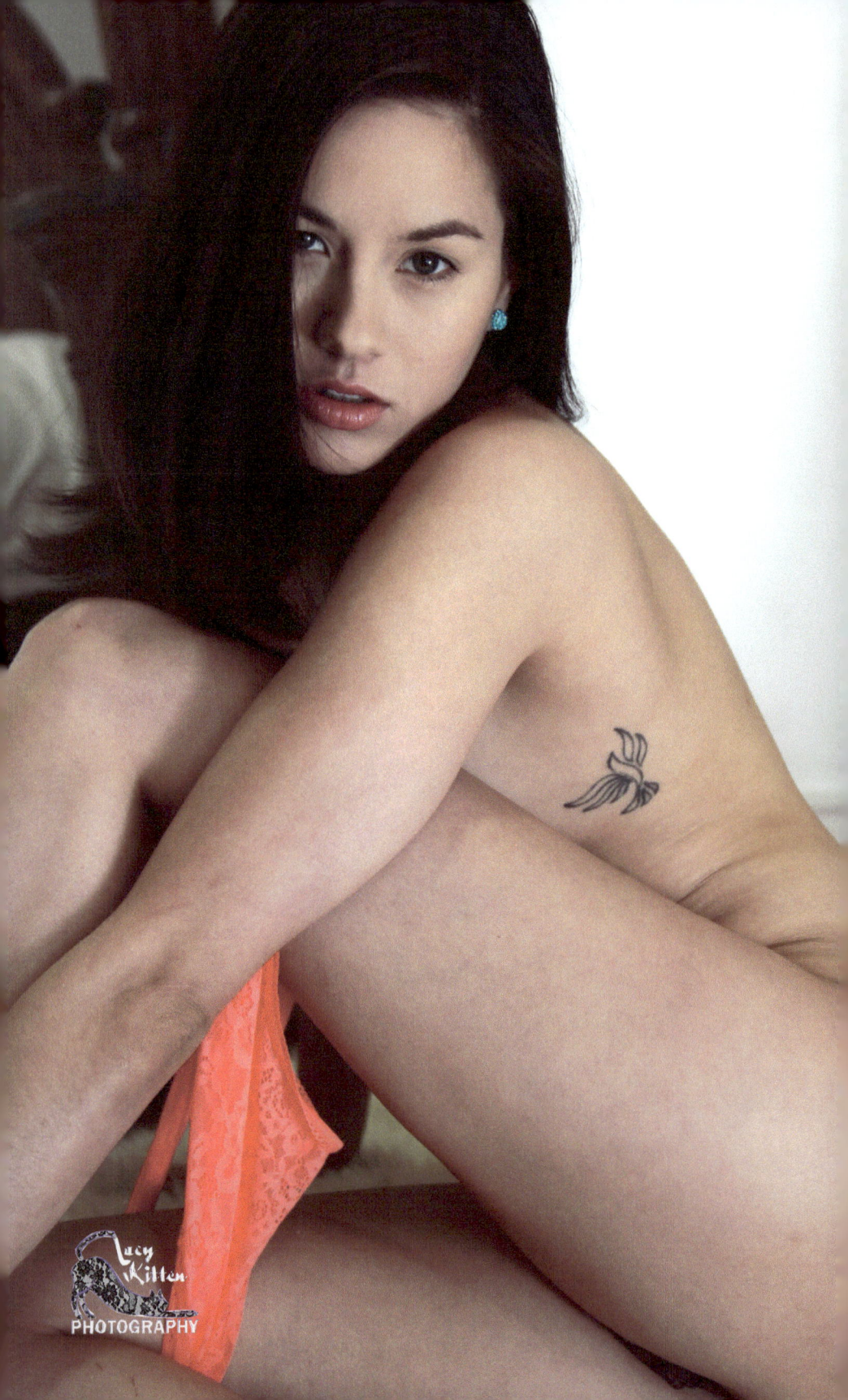

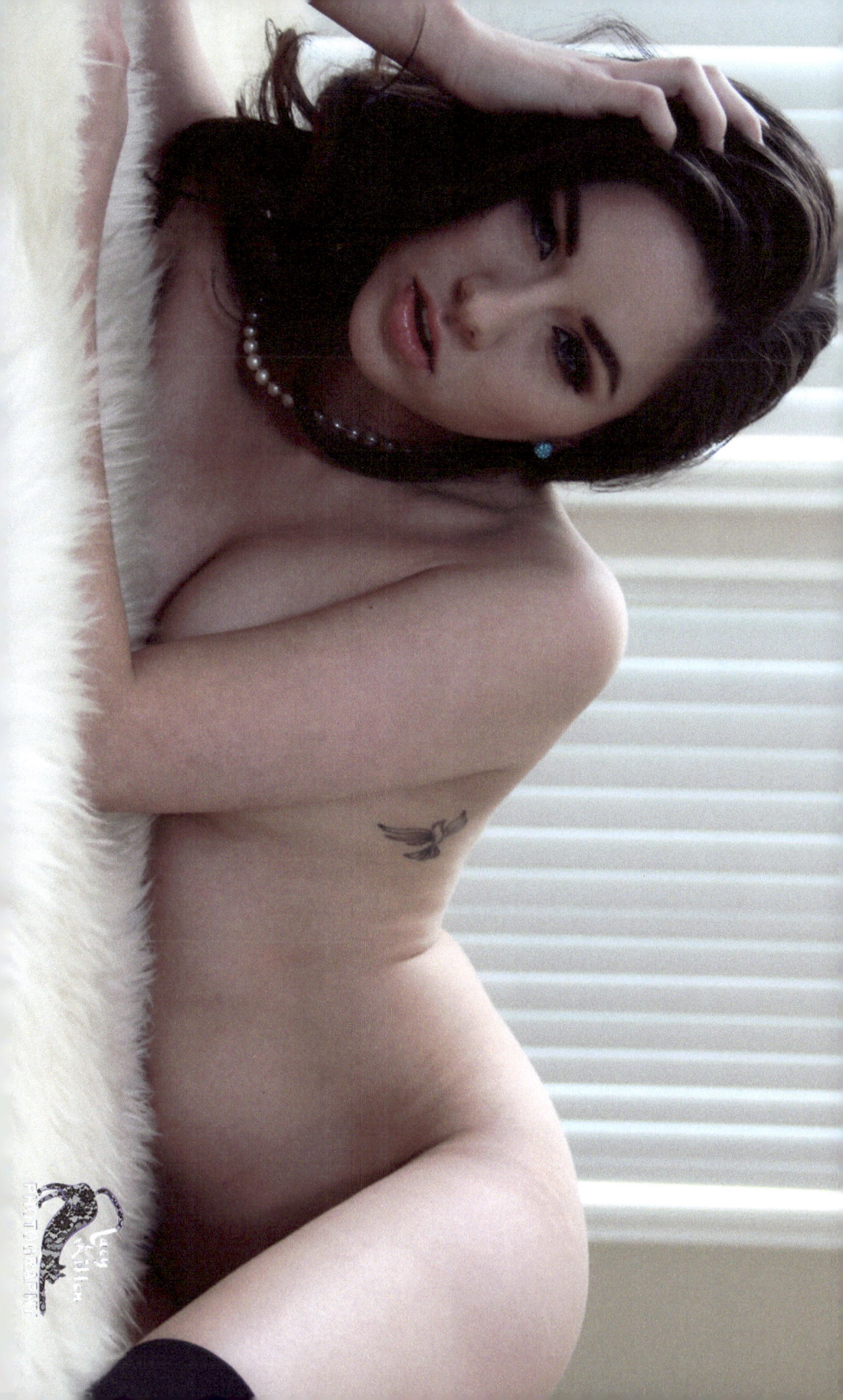

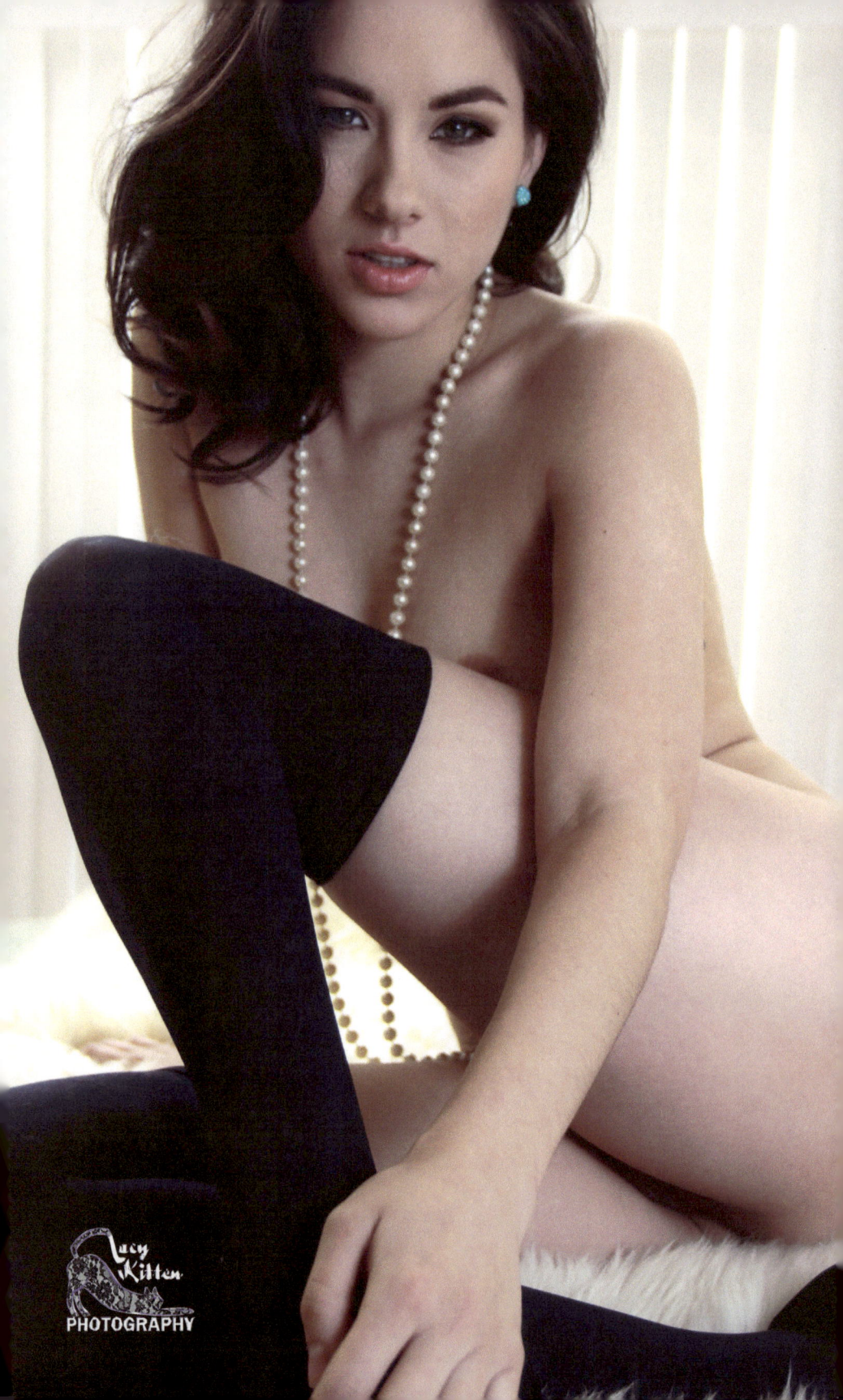

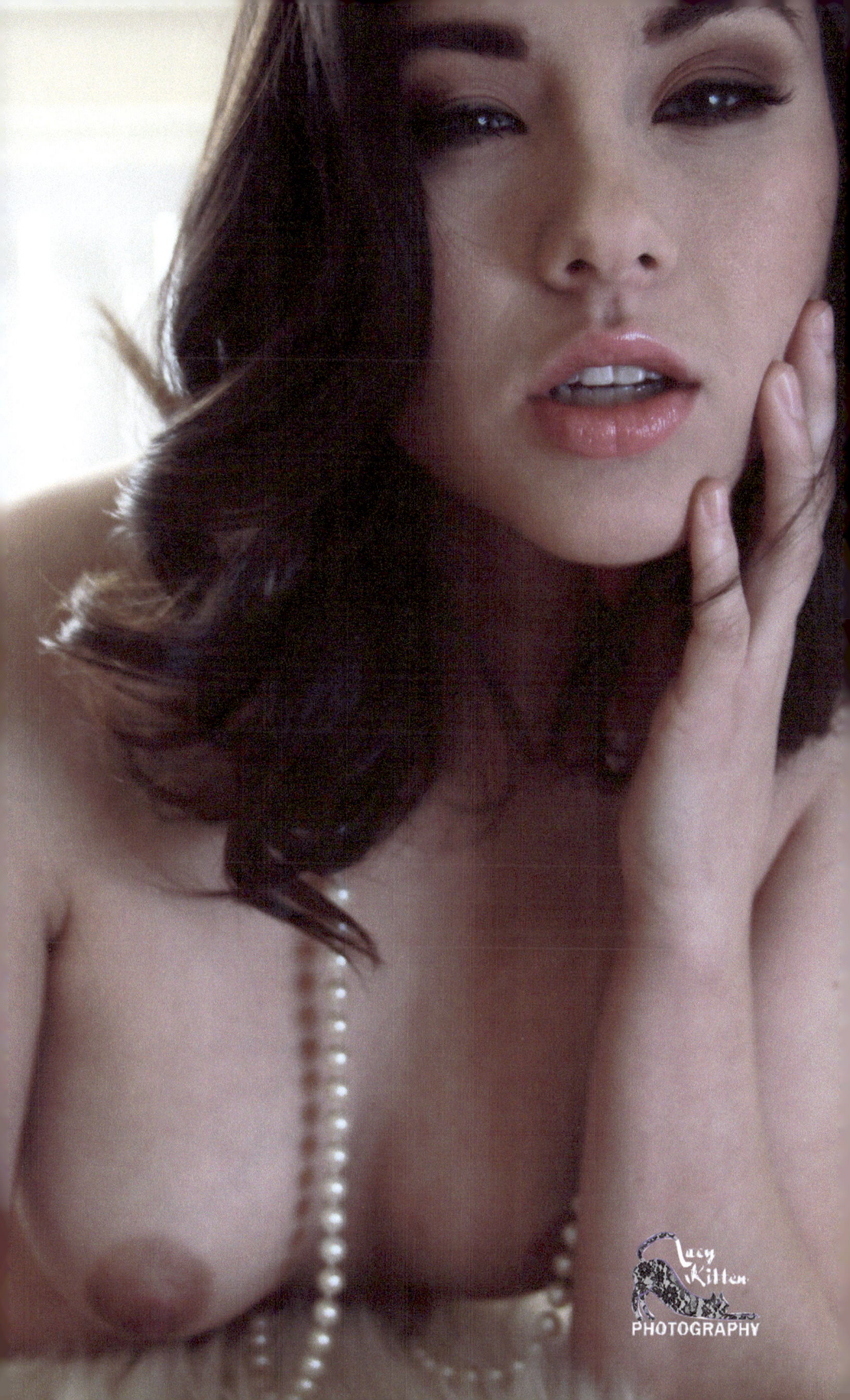

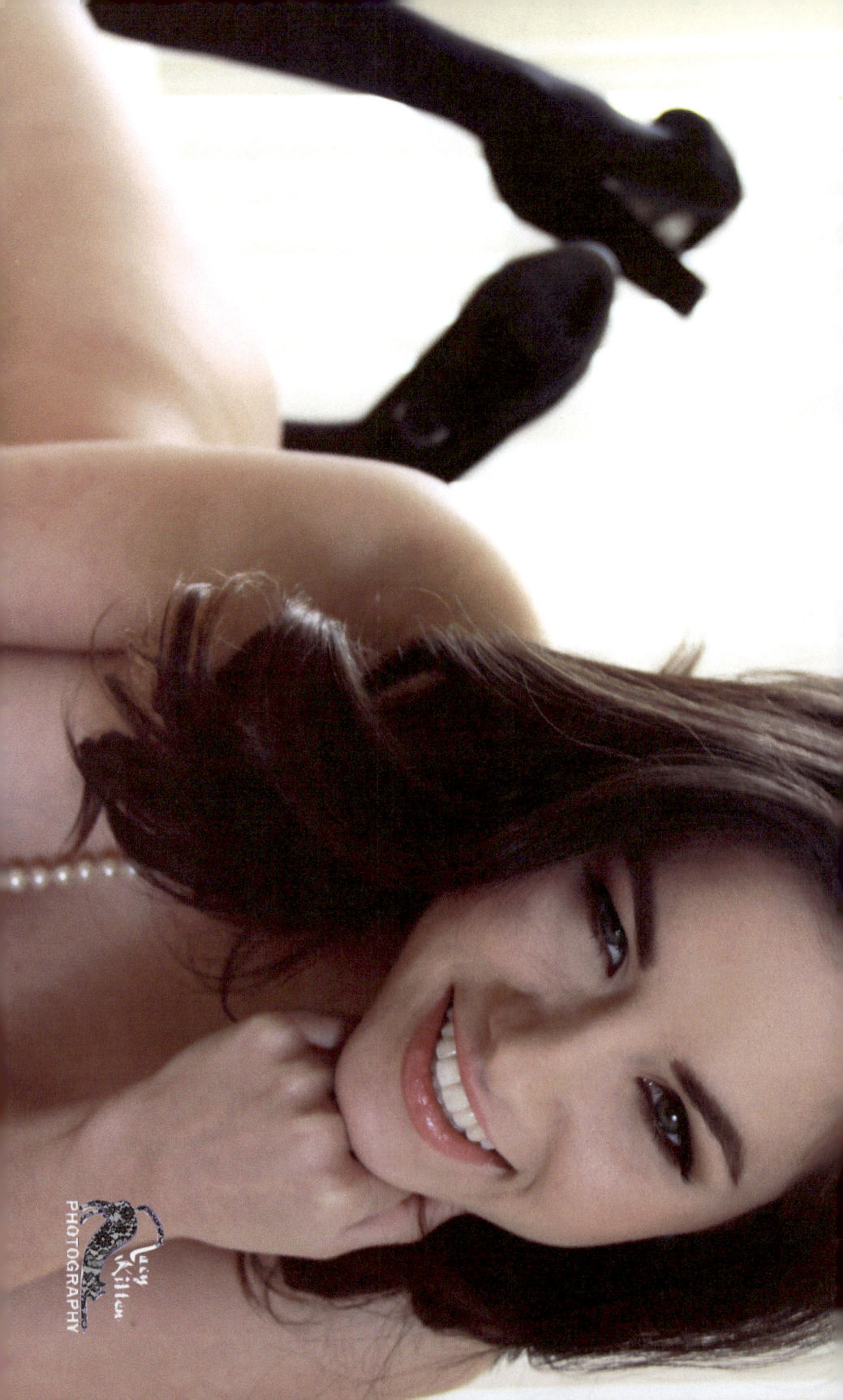

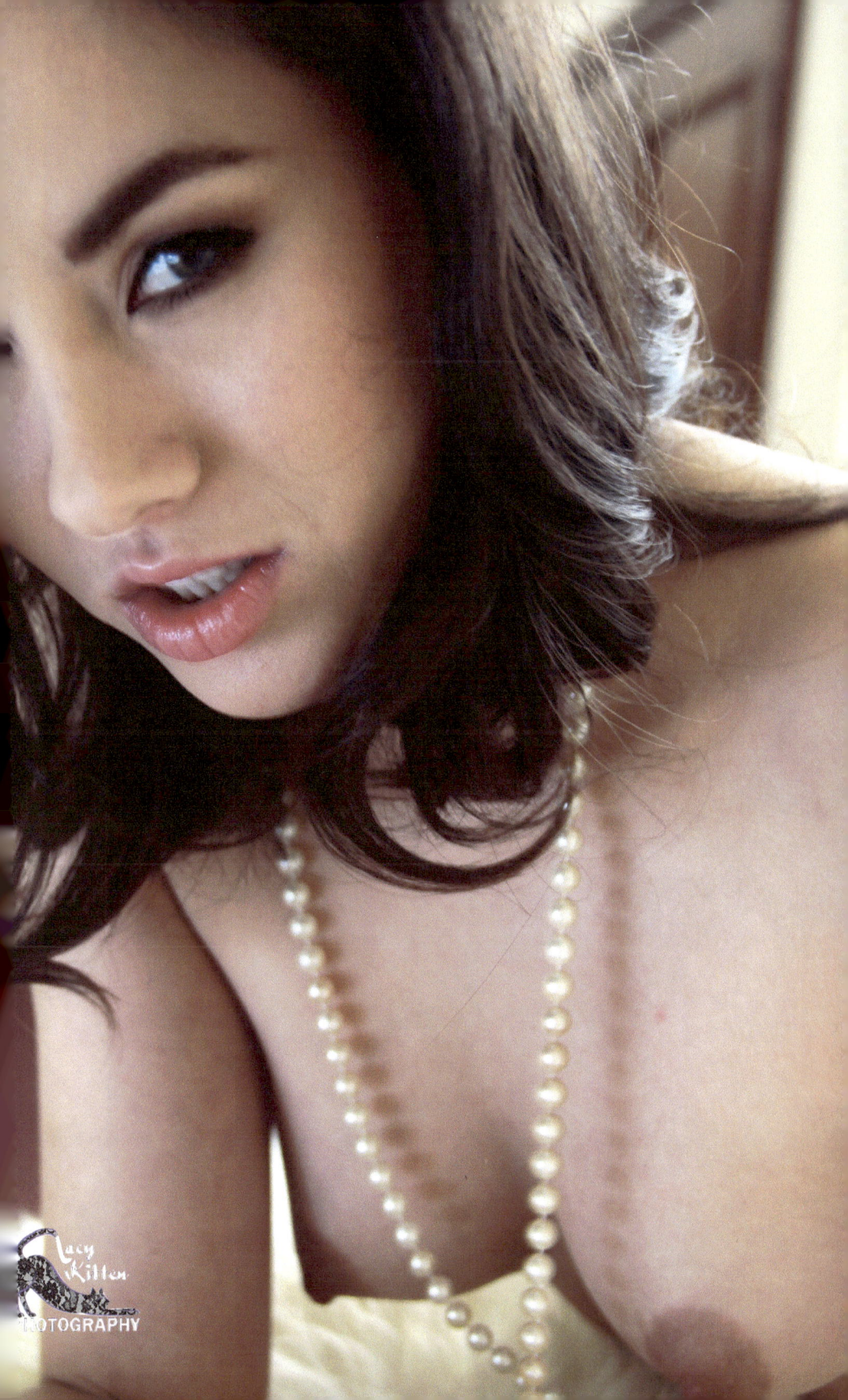

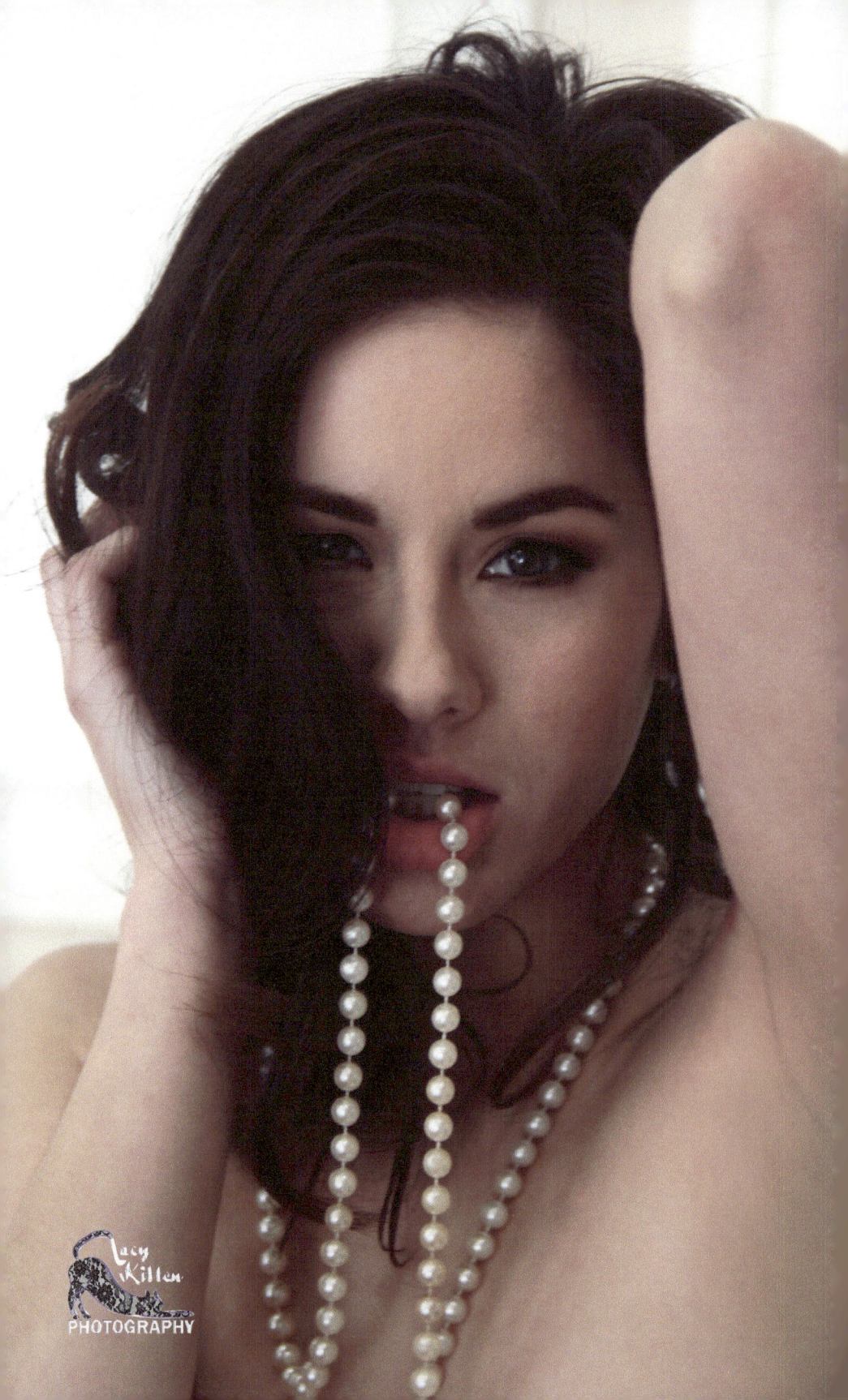

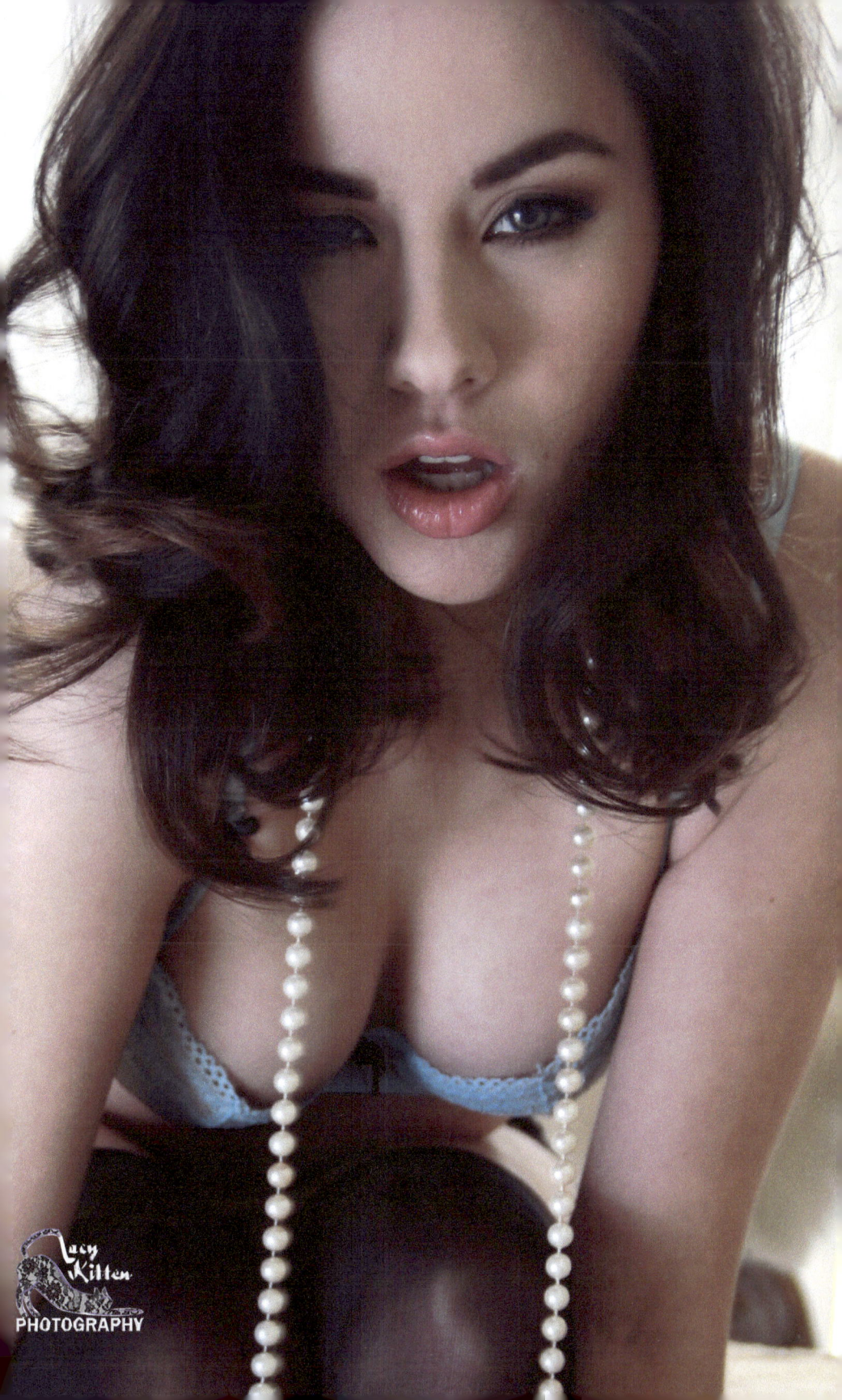

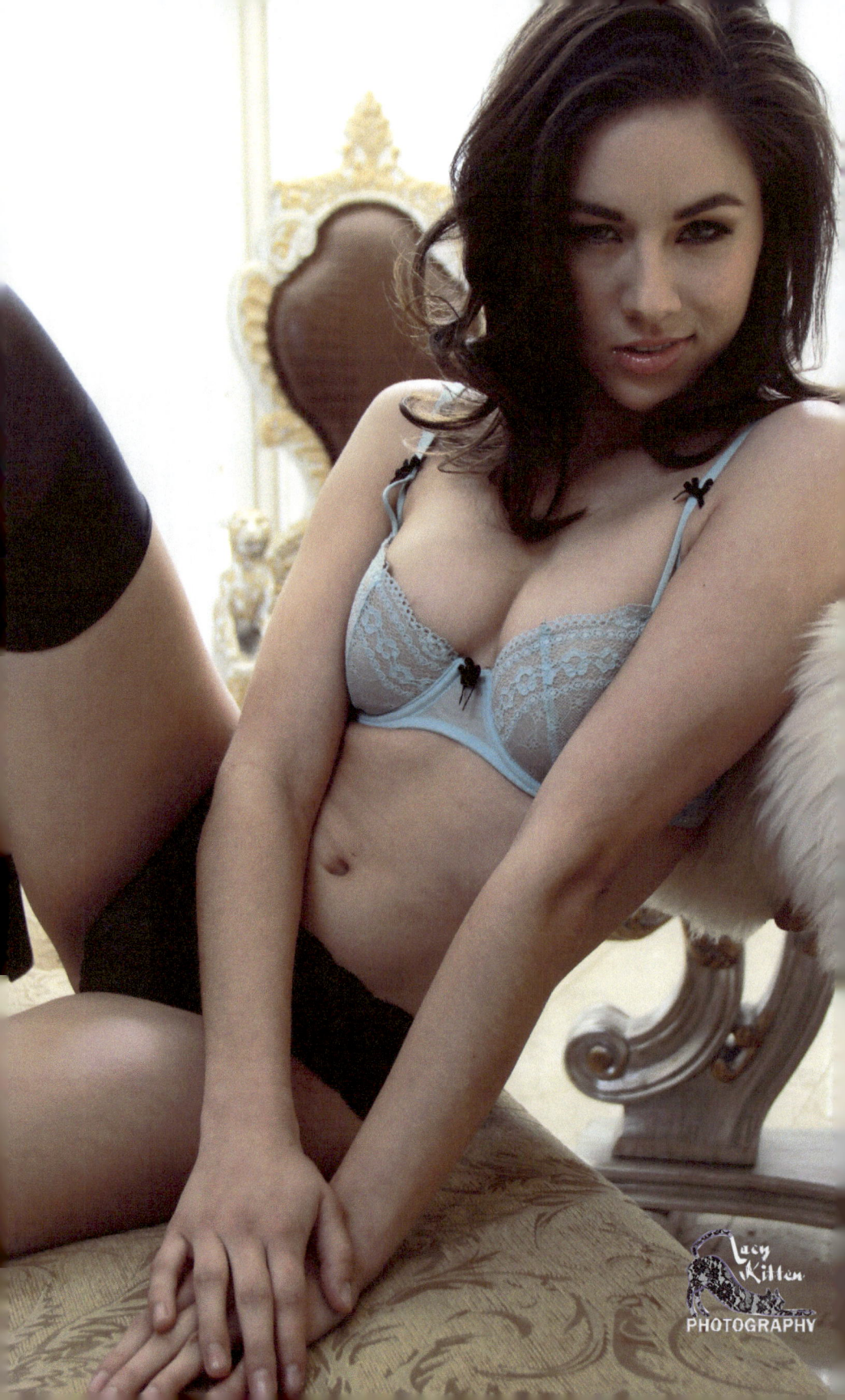

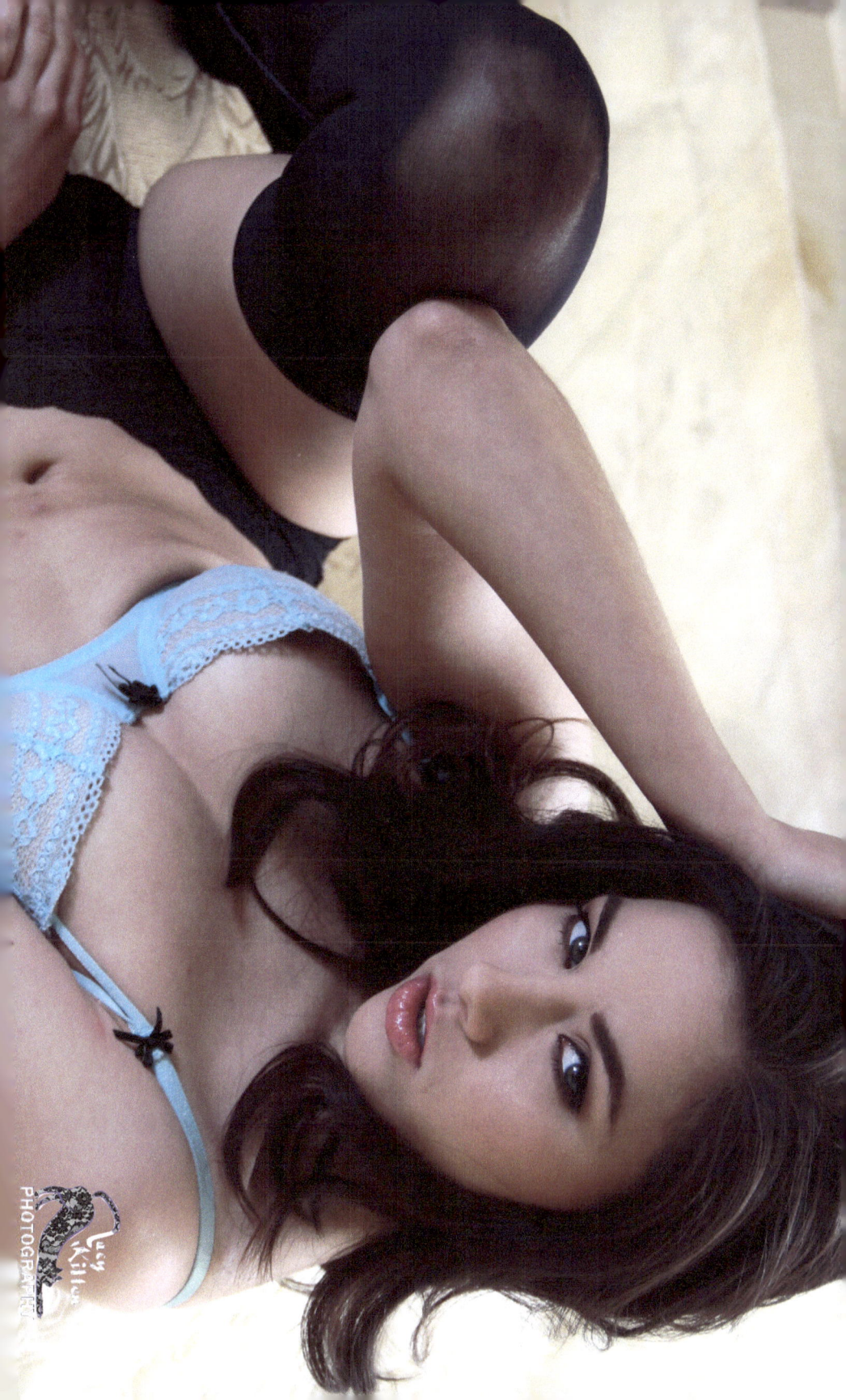

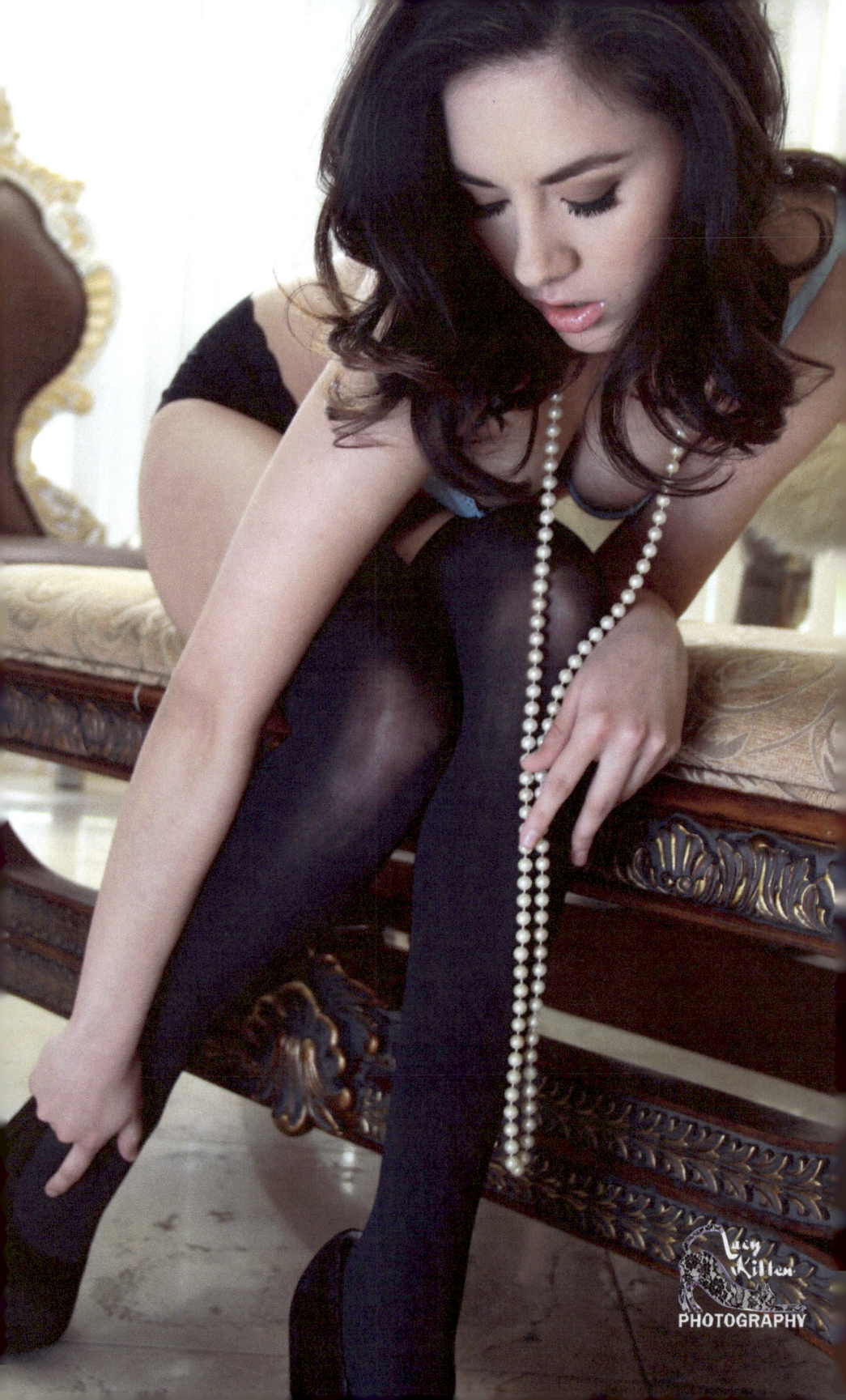

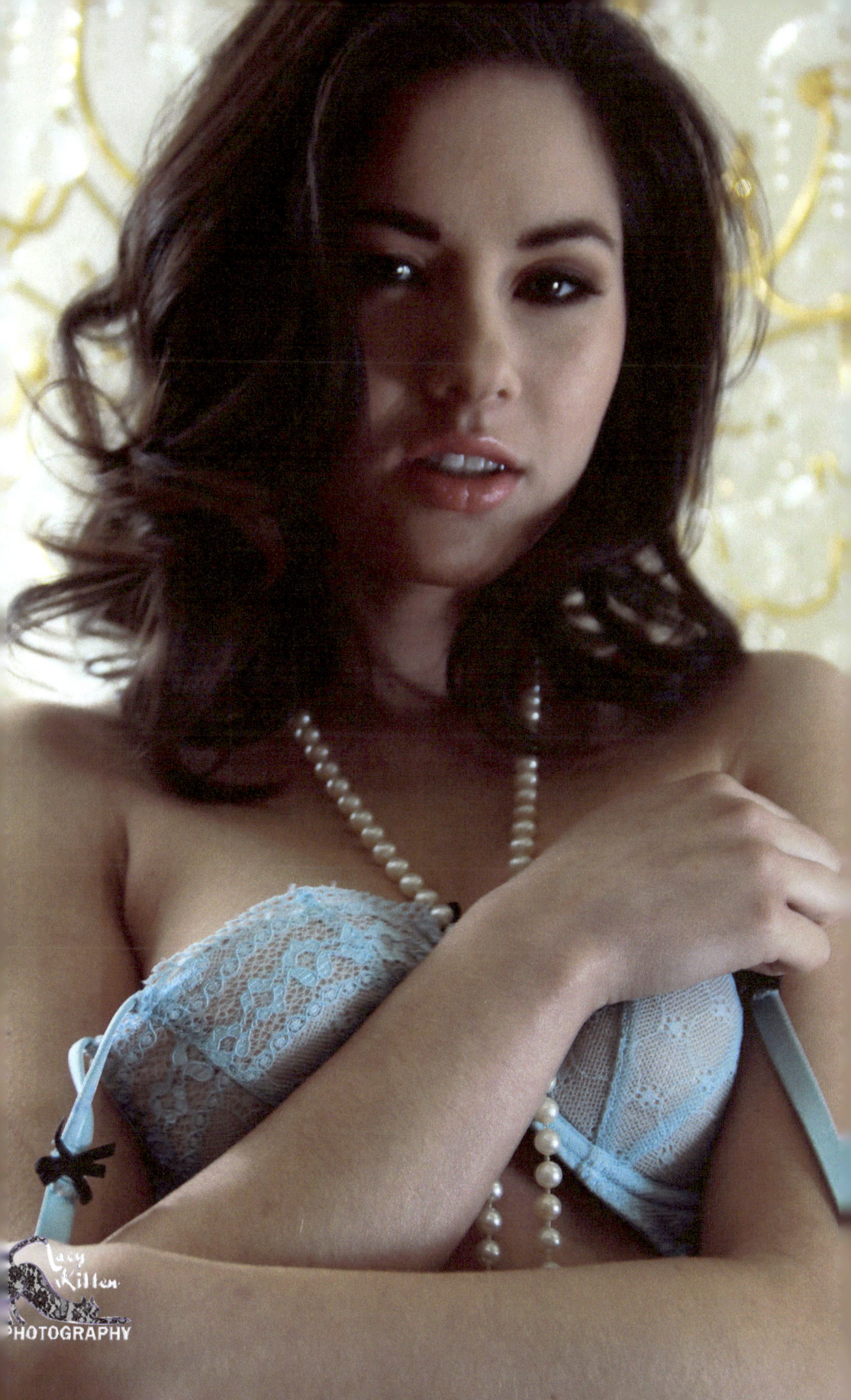

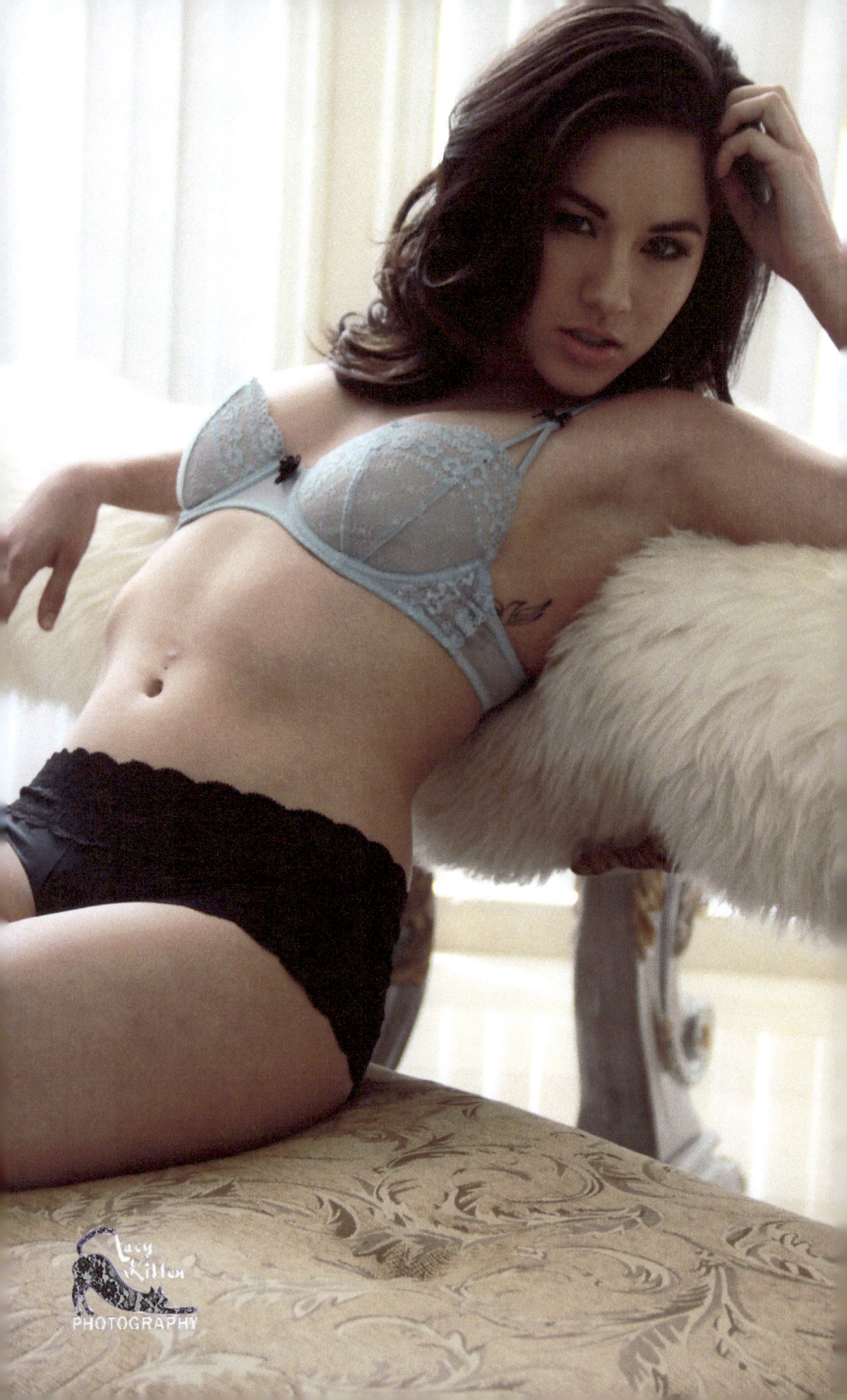

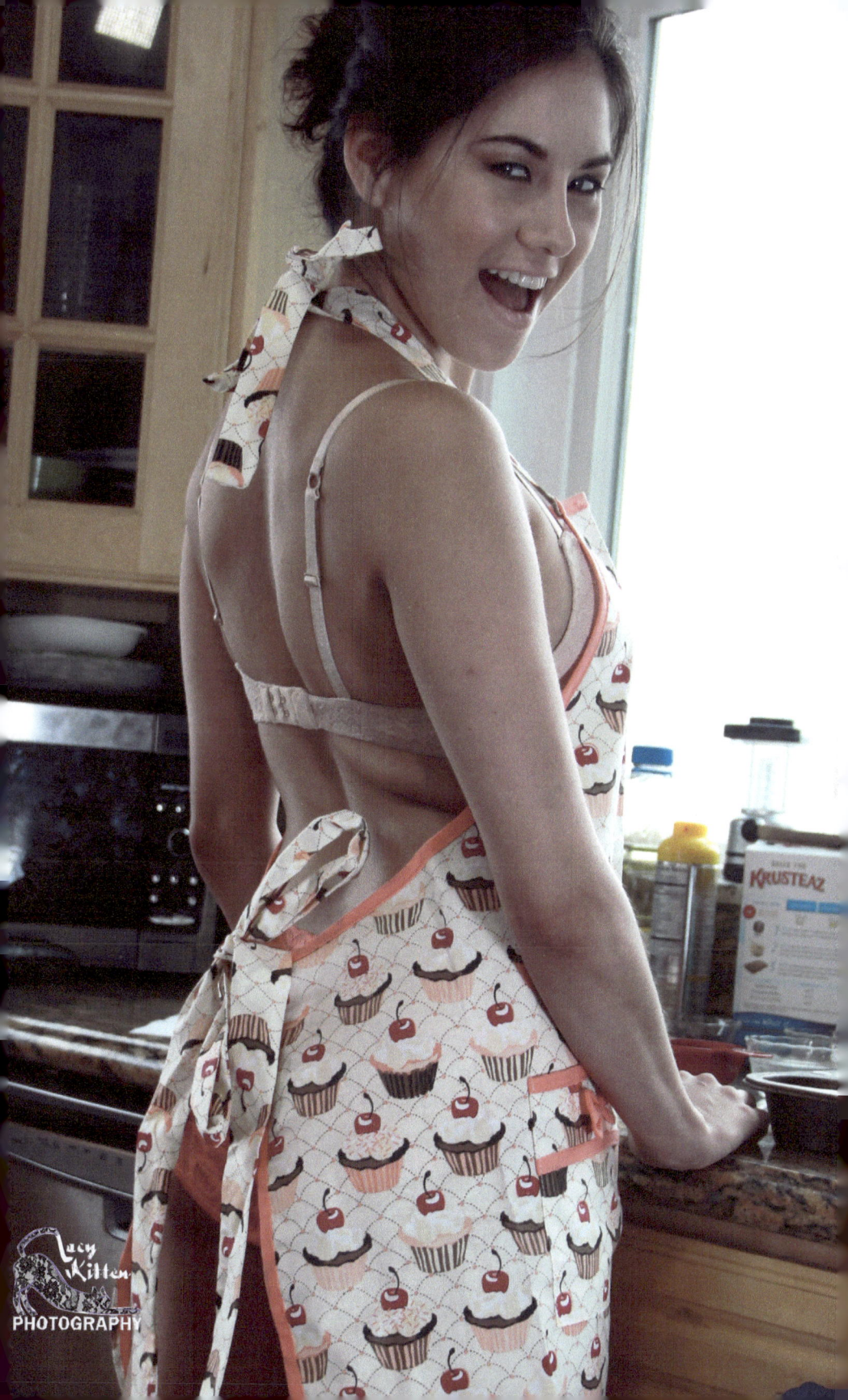

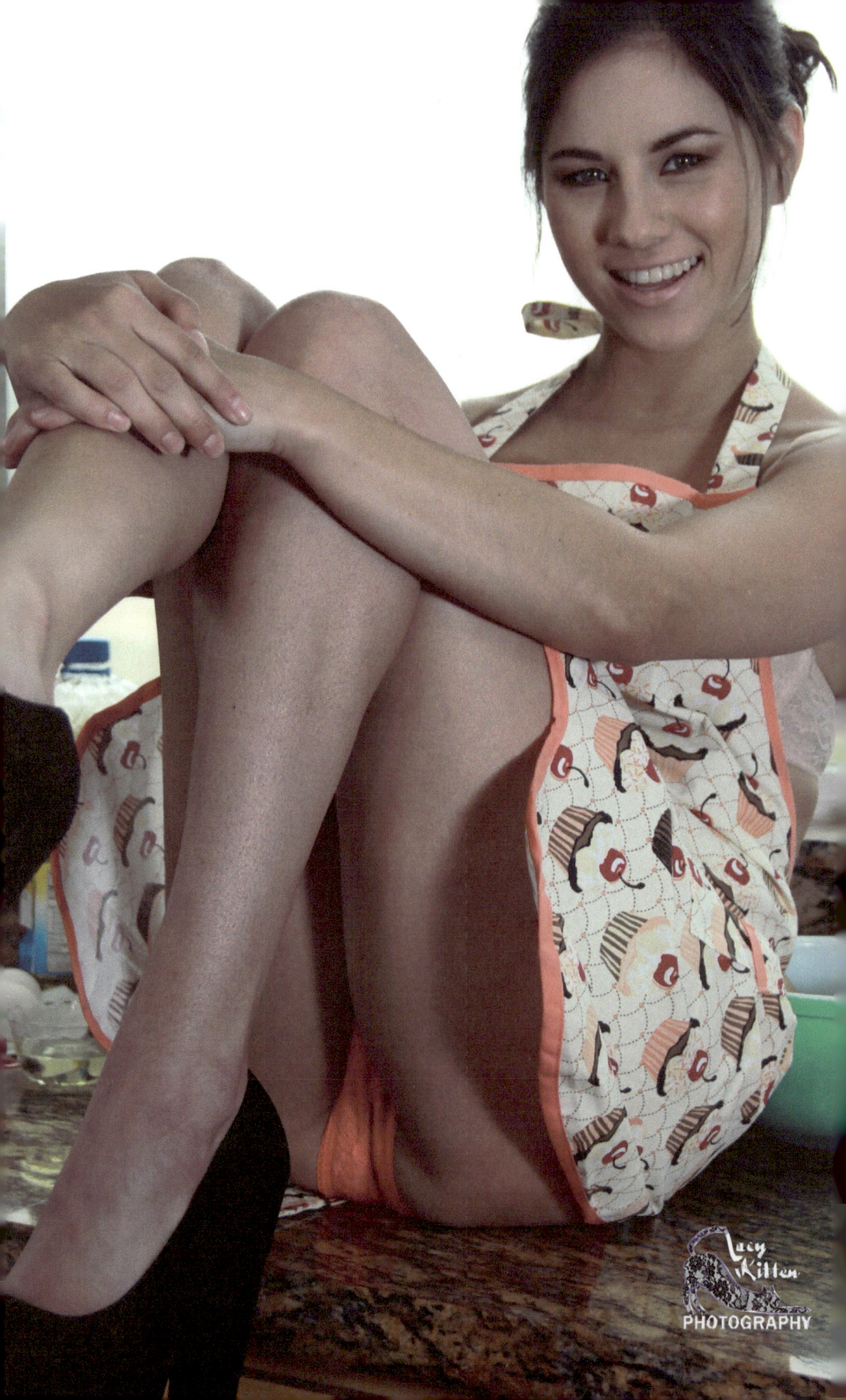

Once upon a time there was a simple girl who loved
taking photographs. Her love developed to
photographs of beautiful sexy women.
Lacy Kitten is a minority in a field dominated by men.
As a woman she brings her feminine perspective
and attention to her erotic photographs,
working with some of the most beautiful models
in the industry. She doesn't just
photograph subjects, she captures a mood.
As an up and coming erotic photographer
she is capturing the attention of the industry
and has an ever growing fan base.

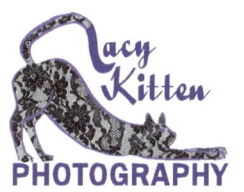

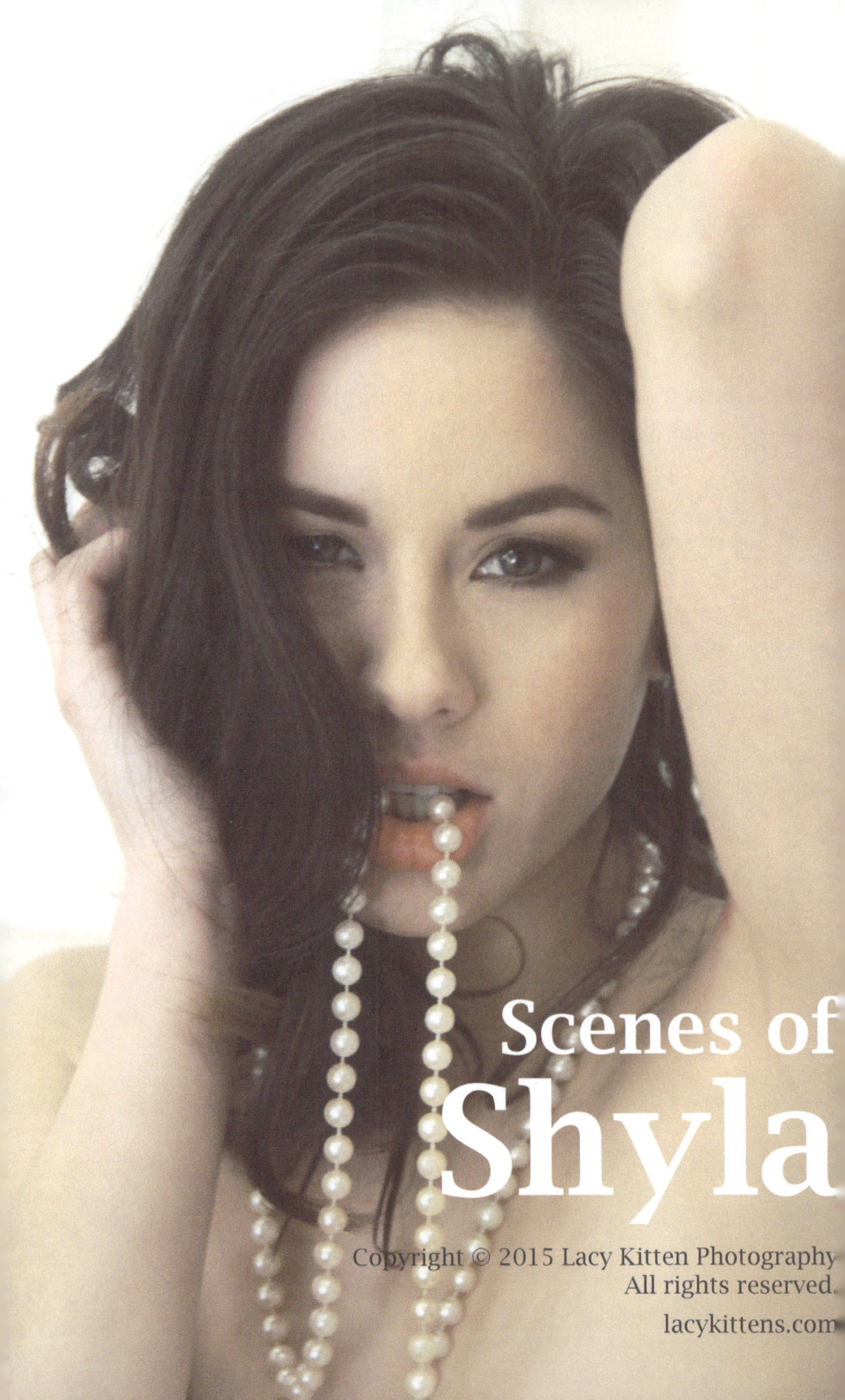

Scenes of
Shyla

www.ingramcontent.com/pod-product-compliance
Lightning Source LLC
Chambersburg PA
CBHW041622180526
45159CB00002BC/975